Helen MacGregor & Stephen

Singing Times Tables

BOOK 2

Songs, chants, raps and games for teaching times tables

CONTENTS

SINGING TIMES TABLES BOOK 2 • HELEN MACGREGOR & STEPHEN CHADWICK © 2013 A&C BLACK PUBLISHERS LTD • www.bloomsbury.com/mus

INTRODUCTION

Singing Times Tables Book 2 is a resource full of motivational and creative ideas for learning and understanding the mathematical processes of times tables through fun songs, chants, raps and games. This book covers all the times tables from two to twelve and is suitable for teaching 7–11 year olds.

As adults, we all know how useful it is to be able to instantly recall and use times tables in everyday situations, from calculating costs when shopping to adjusting measurements for DIY or cookery. If we can learn our tables thoroughly by rote while at school and understand how to apply this knowledge, we have immediate access to them for life!

This resource gives stimulating ideas for aural, visual and kinaesthetic learning through songs, chants and activities that promote:

★ rote learning of the times tables from two to twelve;
★ understanding through exploration and fun, practical maths games;
★ recall of table facts in songs, games and tests;
★ use of a variety of mathematical language.

Cross-curricular links

Many of the songs and chants have cross-curricular links that enable the songs to be integrated into topic work. Each of the times tables songs has a different theme and style, eg *Seven days a week* incorporates use of a calendar and tables calculations based on a frog's life cycle; *Mr Elf* includes ideas for designing sets of Mr Elf's belongings and *Zeros and fives* has a carnival feel. The songs in Section 2 include opportunities for movement and percussion (*Multiples of three*); percussion (*Number lab*) and creating rhyme (*Rhyme time*) to help develop understanding and reinforce learning.

The CD/CD-ROM

There are two parts to the CD – the audio tracks and the graphic resources. The audio tracks section (for use in a conventional CD player) contains a performance track and a backing track for each of the songs, chants or raps (see full track listing on p64). The performance track can be used to help you and the children to learn the song. The backing track allows you to adapt the song or chant and helps to improve memory skills. Many of the songs, chants and raps can, once learnt, also be performed unaccompanied, particularly those that form part of a game.

The CD icons at the top of each activity give the audio track numbers:

 performance track number

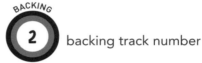 backing track number

The graphic resources section contains the song lyrics and all the relevant times tables charts. It also contains displays, templates and worksheets. All these resources can be printed out or displayed on a whiteboard.

Displays, templates and worksheets

Each song has a photocopiable songsheet that can be used with the children to enhance their literacy skills. A set of photocopiable displays, templates and worksheets that support the activities is included on pages 48–63. All these graphic resources are supplied on the CD/CD-ROM for access on a computer.

The template icons at the top of each activity show the page number where the corresponding template can be found:

 template page number

Teaching focus

The teaching focus of each song, chant or rap can be found at the bottom of each page.

About the activities

The teaching notes give step-by-step suggestions of ways to introduce and teach the songs, chants or raps to the children. It is recommended that the children learn the songs and chants aurally, though you will also want to show them the tables displayed on the songsheets in Section 1.

Extending the activity

Use these ideas to make the activities more challenging, eg by exploring the times table to promote understanding; using and applying the tables knowledge; investigating relationships between tables; or testing recall.

Section 1
Learning the tables

There is a song, chant or rap for each of the times tables appropriate for teaching the age group 7–11. Each song has a different musical style and theme related to the number patterns of the table, eg *Bactrian camel caravan* has an Eastern flavour as the children practise the two times table, counting the procession of camel humps; *Rock with three* is presented in a rock style. The themes can also readily be linked with cross-curricular work.

Section 2
Investigating patterns

These songs, chants or raps provide creative opportunities to explore and understand the mathematical processes of multiplication and division, eg in *Multiples of three* the children create a rhythmical performance piece using the number patterns and relationships of the three, six and nine times tables.

Section 3
Tests

To help ensure the children are confident in their learning of tables facts, these songs give strategies for learning the more tricky times tables as well as plenty of opportunities for testing any times table in fun and engaging ways, eg through a bingo game in *X-men bingo*. You can use the tests flexibly to suit your pupils' needs by differentiating questions for different groups or individuals, or by giving pupils individual worksheets to complete rather than singing the answers out loud as a class.

Bactrian camel caravan

Travel to the desert to see the camel train of Bactrian camels (each with its two humps) appear on the horizon and disappear into the distance. Count the numbers of humps to learn or revise the two times table.

★ Display the songsheet (opposite and CD) and listen to performance track 1 to learn the song.

★ Notice the counting section of multiples of two at the end of the song. As the camels appear, the number of camel humps increases to 24, then as the camels disappear into the distance the humps decrease to 0 again. You may like to perform this with a *crescendo* (gradually louder) and *diminuendo* (gradually quieter) for dramatic effect!

EXTENDING THE ACTIVITY

★ Illustrate the number pattern of the two times table by creating a dance performance of the camel train.

★ Ask twelve pairs of children to find a way to create a two-humped camel, eg the child in front forms a camel's head and neck with one arm held high, while the heads of both children become the camel's humps.

★ As you sing the song each 'camel' joins the train, moving in time to the music. Appoint a camel train driver to count the camels and humps during the times table section of the song.

WHAT YOU WILL NEED

★ An enlarged copy of the songsheet (opposite and CD)

Extension activity:

★ A large space in order to travel in a line

Teaching focus
• Learning and exploring the two times table.

SINGING TIMES TABLES BOOK 2 • HELEN MACGREGOR & STEPHEN CHADWICK © 2013 A&C BLACK PUBLISHERS LTD • www.bloomsbury.com/music

Bactrian camel caravan

A caravan of camels, twelve two-humped, hairy mammals.
Across the desert travel on bumpy Bactrian camels.

$0 \times 2 = 0$
$1 \times 2 = 2$
$2 \times 2 = 4$
$3 \times 2 = 6$
$4 \times 2 = 8$
$5 \times 2 = 10$
$6 \times 2 = 12$
$7 \times 2 = 14$
$8 \times 2 = 16$
$9 \times 2 = 18$
$10 \times 2 = 20$
$11 \times 2 = 22$
$12 \times 2 = 24$

Twenty-four camel humps in a row!

A caravan of camels, twelve two-humped, hairy mammals.
Across the desert travel on bumpy Bactrian camels.

0 2 4 6 8 10 12 14 16 18 20 22 24

24 22 20 18 16 14 12 10 8 6 4 2 0

Rock with three

Learn the three times table with this rock number for aspiring air guitarists!

★ Display the songsheet (opposite and CD) and follow the three times table as you listen to performance track 3 to learn the melody. All join in with the chanted multiples sequence at the end after 'Rock with'.

★ Play the performance track again and join in with the whole song:

> Zero times three is zero,
> One times three is three…

EXTENDING THE ACTIVITY

★ Show the class the air guitar display (p48 and CD). Instead of chanting the multiples of three in the 'Rock with' section, chant the consecutive numbers between each multiple in groups of three, starting with 0 1 2 and continuing up to 36. Pause after each group of numbers.

Play air guitar as you count, giving one strum for each of the consecutive numbers or move the guitar up, down and up again.

★ Instead of playing air guitar, add different sets of body percussion to the number groups, eg

Clapping:	0	1	2	(rest)
Stamping:	3	4	5	(rest)
Clicking:	6	7	8	(rest)

★ Divide the class into two groups: group 1 chants the multiples (0 3 6 9 etc) while group 2 chants the consecutive numbers.

Transfer this onto two types of percussion instrument, eg group 1 plays drums, group 2 plays claves. Perform the whole song, adding the percussion instruments to the 'Rock with' section.

WHAT YOU WILL NEED

★ An enlarged version of the songsheet (opposite and CD)

Extension activity:

★ Air guitar display (p48 and CD)

★ Two types of percussion instrument, eg drums and claves

Teaching focus
• Learning and exploring the three times table.

Rock with three

0 x 3 = 0
1 x 3 = 3
2 x 3 = 6
3 x 3 = 9
4 x 3 = 12
5 x 3 = 15
6 x 3 = 18
7 x 3 = 21
8 x 3 = 24
9 x 3 = 27
10 x 3 = 30
11 x 3 = 33
12 x 3 = 36

Now come and rock with me,
Get ready with your air guitar,
Rock with three,
Rock with:

0 3 6 9 12 15 18 21 24 27 30 33 36

Four beat bars

Learn the four times table and its multiples by alternately rapping along to the music and clapping four beats.

★ Display the songsheet (opposite and CD) where everyone can see it. Play performance track 5 and all join in singing and rapping the times table:

> Sing: Zero times four is zero,
> One times four is four,
> Rap: Two times four is eight,
> Three times four is twelve...

Finish by rapping the multiples: 0 4 8...

EXTENDING THE ACTIVITY

★ Split into two groups and show the class the Extension activity display (p49 and CD).
Group 1: sings and raps the times table
Group 2: shakes hands in the air four times after group 1 has rapped *0 x 4 = 0*, saying '*zero*' on each shake. After each subsequent sum, group 2 counts the four consecutive numbers between each mulitple, eg *1 2 3 4*, clapping on each number.

Swap groups so that everyone has the opportunity to perform both parts.

★ Divide the class into small groups. Each group devises other four-beat body percussion patterns to perform with the counting section, eg stamp, knees, click click.

All perform the group 1 part together, then alternate with all the small groups as they count and perform their own body percussion on the count up.

★ To check the children's times tables knowledge and investigate its number pattern, give each child a copy of the ten-point circle template (p50 and CD). The children plot the four times table to make a 'mystic rose' (see opposite).

Ask them to write down the four times table, then plot and draw straight lines to join the units of the multiples of four on the points of the circle: 4 8 12 16...

★ Compare the four times table 'mystic rose' with a circle pattern based on the two times table, or with other times tables.

WHAT YOU WILL NEED

★ An enlarged version of the songsheet (opposite and CD)

Extension activity:

★ Extension activity display (p49 and CD)

★ Mystic rose template for each child (p50 and CD)

★ Pens

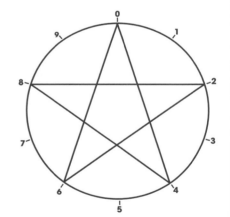

Teaching focus
• Learning and exploring the four times table.

SINGING TIMES TABLES BOOK 2 • HELEN MACGREGOR & STEPHEN CHADWICK © 2013 A&C BLACK PUBLISHERS LTD • www.bloomsbury.com/mus

Four beat bars

Sing: 0 x 4 = 0

           1 x 4 = 4

Rap: 2 x 4 = 8

           3 x 4 = 12

           4 x 4 = 16

           5 x 4 = 20

Sing: 6 x 4 = 24

           7 x 4 = 28

Rap: 8 x 4 = 32

           9 x 4 = 36

          10 x 4 = 40

          11 x 4 = 44

Sing: 12 x 4 = 48

Rap:

0 4 8 12 16 20 24 28 32 36 40 44 48

Zeros and fives

Come down to the carnival and dance with the reggae beat as you sing and rap to memorise the five times table in increasing and decreasing order.

★ Display the songsheet (opposite and CD) and practise saying the five times table from *0 x 5* to *12 x 5*, then work your way back down to *0 x 5*:

> *Twelve times five is sixty,*
> *Eleven times five is fifty-five…*

★ Play performance track 7 and sing and rap the times table as it becomes familiar. Learn the words and melody of the chorus and add this to the beginning and end of the song.

★ Finally, perform the whole song with backing track 8.

WHAT YOU WILL NEED

★ An enlarged version of the songsheet (opposite and CD)

EXTENDING THE ACTIVITY

★ Choose six children to stand in a line facing the class. The children may suggest some simple dance moves to perform on the spot with the song, eg roll hands then open and shake to one side, roll and shake to the other side.

★ Ask the children to investigate and describe the number patterns in the table, eg the multiples alternate between odd and even numbers: 5 10 15 20…; the unit digits alternate between 5 and 0.

★ Can they think of a 'tables trick' to help them calculate when multiplying by five?

The five times table is half the ten times table, so you can multiply the number by ten (add a zero) then halve the answer, eg

Sum: $24 \times 5 = ?$
Step 1: $24 \times 10 = 240$
Step 2: $240 \div 2 = 120$
Therefore: $24 \times 5 = 120$

Teaching focus
• Learning and exploring the five times table.

Zeros and fives

Sing: The five times table
Is easy to create,
'Cos the fives and zeros
Love to alternate!

Rap: $0 \times 5 = 0$
$1 \times 5 = 5$

$2 \times 5 = 10$
$3 \times 5 = 15$

Sing: $4 \times 5 = 20$
$5 \times 5 = 25$
$6 \times 5 = 30$
$7 \times 5 = 35$

Rap: $8 \times 5 = 40$
$9 \times 5 = 45$

$10 \times 5 = 50$
$11 \times 5 = 55$

Sing: $12 \times 5 = 60$
$11 \times 5 = 55$
$10 \times 5 = 50$
$9 \times 5 = 45$

Rap: $8 \times 5 = 40$
$7 \times 5 = 35$

$6 \times 5 = 30$
$5 \times 5 = 25$

Sing: $4 \times 5 = 20$
$3 \times 5 = 15$
$2 \times 5 = 10$
$1 \times 5 = 5$
$0 \times 5 = 0$

Chant: 0   5   10   15
20   25   30   35
40   45   50   55   60

Sing: The five times table
Is easy to create,
'Cos the fives and zeros
Love to alternate!

Recap, rap, clap

PERFORMANCE **9**   BACKING **10**

Sing Recap, rap and clap to learn the six times table. The table is divided into sections, each one is sung then recapped in the rap. The syllables of each multiple are clapped, eg 1 x 6 = 6 (clap), 7 x 6 = 42 (clap clap clap).

★ Display the songsheet (opposite and CD). Play performance track 9 to listen to the tune of the sung sections. Notice that each sung section is repeated as a rap.

★ Listen again and in the rap sections add silent hand shakes for zero and clap the syllables of the other multiples.

★ Perform the whole song with backing track 10.

★ Divide into two groups. Group 1 sings and group 2 raps and claps.

Repeat, swapping parts so that everyone has the opportunity to lead and recap.

WHAT YOU WILL NEED

★ An enlarged version of the songsheet (opposite and CD)

EXTENDING THE ACTIVITY

★ As an extension to the previous group activity, group 1 mixes up the sums, deciding beforehand on an order. Group 2 must copy by rapping and clapping the new order, eg

Group 1 (sing): *1 x 6 = 6*   *7 x 6 = 42*

Group 2 (rap): *1 x 6 = 6*   *7 x 6 = 42*

★ Ask the children to investigate the number patterns of the six times table. Can they find patterns to help them multiply by six? Here is an example:

~ Look at the multiples in the five times table (5 10 15 20 etc) and add as follows to get the multiples of the six times table:

```
 5 +  1 =  6
10 +  2 = 12
15 +  3 = 18
20 +  4 = 24...
```

Teaching focus
• Learning and exploring the six times table.

Recap, rap, clap

Group 1 (sing):

$$0 \times 6 = 0$$
$$1 \times 6 = 6$$
$$2 \times 6 = 12$$
$$3 \times 6 = 18$$

Group 2 (rap):

$$0 \times 6 = 0$$
$$1 \times 6 = 6$$
$$2 \times 6 = 12$$
$$3 \times 6 = 18$$

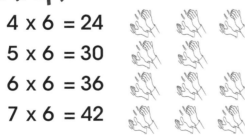

Group 1 (sing):

$$4 \times 6 = 24$$
$$5 \times 6 = 30$$
$$6 \times 6 = 36$$
$$7 \times 6 = 42$$

Group 2 (rap):

$$4 \times 6 = 24$$
$$5 \times 6 = 30$$
$$6 \times 6 = 36$$
$$7 \times 6 = 42$$

Group 1 (sing):

$$8 \times 6 = 48$$
$$9 \times 6 = 54$$
$$10 \times 6 = 60$$
$$11 \times 6 = 66$$

Group 2 (rap):

$$8 \times 6 = 48$$
$$9 \times 6 = 54$$
$$10 \times 6 = 60$$
$$11 \times 6 = 66$$

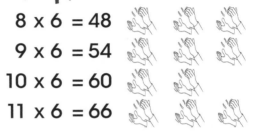

Group 1 (sing):

$$12 \times 6 = 72$$

Group 2 (rap):

$$12 \times 6 = 72$$

Seven days a week

Listen to the wiggling tadpoles growing into frogs as you learn the seven times table. Calculate the number of days it takes in the typical life cycle of a frog to change from egg to tadpole and reach adult frog stage at twelve weeks!

★ Display the songsheet (opposite and CD) and follow the times table as you listen to performance track 11.

★ Play the performance track again and sing along with the seven times table:

> *Zero times seven is zero,*
> *One times seven is seven…*

At the end, chant the multiples of seven from 0 to 84, giving you the total number of days in the frog's life cycle.

EXTENDING THE ACTIVITY

★ Using a blank twelve-week calendar and the frog life cycle diagram (pp51–52 and CD), explore the life cycle of a frog and plot its development on the twelve-week calendar. Calculate and decide on the typical number of days and weeks in each stage, eg between one and three weeks the eggs hatch; after a week the tadpoles start to swim; after four weeks the gills form; legs appear at six to nine weeks, by twelve weeks the tail has become a stump and the frog is an adult.

★ Use the calendar to calculate the answers to tables questions, eg

  ~ How many days is the frogspawn in the pond if the tadpole hatches at two weeks? (2 weeks x 7 days = 14 days)

  ~ How many days does the frog have legs during its first twelve weeks if they grow at seven weeks? (5 weeks x 7 days = 35 days)

★ You may like to plot other events on the calendar and set the class calculations for testing the seven times table.

WHAT YOU WILL NEED

★ An enlarged version of the songsheet (opposite and CD)

For the Extension activity:

★ A blank twelve-week calendar (p51 and CD)

★ Frog life cycle diagram (p52 and CD)

Teaching focus
• Learning and exploring the seven times table.

Seven days a week

$0 \times 7 = 0$

$1 \times 7 = 7$

$2 \times 7 = 14$

$3 \times 7 = 21$

$4 \times 7 = 28$

$5 \times 7 = 35$

$6 \times 7 = 42$

$7 \times 7 = 49$

$8 \times 7 = 56$

$9 \times 7 = 63$

$10 \times 7 = 70$

$11 \times 7 = 77$

$12 \times 7 = 84$

0   7   14   21   28   35   42   49   56   63   70   77   84

Octopi

While swimming and exploring deep underwater, the diver strays into an area where octopi live. As each octopus appears, it wraps its eight tentacles around the diver. Count the tentacles the diver has to escape from if he is going to survive!

★ Play performance track 13 to learn the chorus, then all sing the eight times table using the songsheet (opposite and CD), or from memory:

> *Zero times eight is zero,*
> *One times eight is eight…*

At the end, join in with the multiples of eight.

EXTENDING THE ACTIVITY

★ This time the diver descends and meets a different number of octopi at each new depth. Make a diver (p53 and CD) and ask the children to make individual cut-out octopi using the templates (p53 and CD), or their own design. They will need 78 octopi in total.

Make a vertical depth chart with a mark at every metre starting at 0 for surface level and ending at 12. Next to each depth mark add a different number of octopi from zero to twelve in a mixed order (eg at the first level there are seven octopi, at the second level there are three octopi). The maximum number of octopi at any level should be twelve.

Use the diver to indicate the depth level. The children need to multiply the number of octopi at each depth level by the number of tentacles (ie eight). Use the chart to practise the times table in this mixed order, eg

Surface level:	*Zero times eight is zero,*
First level:	*Seven times eight is fifty-six, (ie 7 octopi x 8 tentacles = 56)*
Second level:	*Three times eight is twenty-four,*
Third level:	*Nine times eight is seventy-two...*

At the end, can the children recall the multiples (ie total number of tentacles) in the matching order by looking at the different numbers of octopi placed on the chart (eg 0 16 64)?

WHAT YOU WILL NEED

★ An enlarged version of the songsheet (opposite and CD)

Extension activity:

★ Materials to make a diving frieze

★ 78 octopi and a diver (p53 and CD)

★ Paints and other decorating materials if the children are making their own octopi

Teaching focus
• Learning and exploring the eight times table.

Octopi

Chorus:

Octopi, the octopi, they're coming to get me, the octopi!
Octopi, the octopi, their tentacles grab me,
I'm going to die!

0 x 8 = 0
1 x 8 = 8
2 x 8 = 16
3 x 8 = 24
4 x 8 = 32
5 x 8 = 40
6 x 8 = 48
7 x 8 = 56
8 x 8 = 64
9 x 8 = 72
10 x 8 = 80
11 x 8 = 88
12 x 8 = 96

Chorus

0 8 16 24 32 40 48 56 64 72 80 88 96

Cloud nine

PERFORMANCE **15**   BACKING **16**

The children will be walking on cloud nine when they memorise the nine times table using this song and rap! The chorus helps them to remember the pattern of numbers in the table, before rapping the times table and its multiples.

★ Display the songsheet (opposite and CD) and ask the children to describe the patterns they notice in the multiples, eg the units decrease in sequence, the tens increase; the digits add up to nine.

★ Teach them the first chorus using performance track 15, ensuring that they understand each description of the patterns of digits, units and tens referred to in the lyrics.

★ Rap the times table and multiples sections, then perform the whole song with backing track 16.

EXTENDING THE ACTIVITY

★ Can the children find other helpful ways to multiply by nine? (See the *Nine times table finger trick*, pp34–35, for a method of checking the table up to 10 x 9 using the fingers of both hands.)

★ Multiply the number by ten then subtract the number you are multiplying from the total, eg

Sum:	7 x 9 =	?
Step 1:	7 x 10 =	70
Step 2:	70 - 7 =	63
Answer:	7 x 9 =	63

Try this with bigger numbers, eg

Sum:	25 x 9 =	?
Step 1:	25 x 10 =	250
Step 2:	250 - 25 =	225
Answer:	25 x 9 =	225

WHAT YOU WILL NEED

★ An enlarged version of the songsheet (opposite and CD)

Teaching focus
• Learning and exploring the nine times table.

Cloud nine

Chorus:

I'm walking on cloud nine, where numbers shine,
The digits in the answers always make a number 9.
Add 10 to the tens, you'll see the light,
Take one from the units and you will get it right.

$0 \times 9 = 0$
$1 \times 9 = 9$
$2 \times 9 = 18$
$3 \times 9 = 27$
$4 \times 9 = 36$
$5 \times 9 = 45$
$6 \times 9 = 54$
$7 \times 9 = 63$
$8 \times 9 = 72$
$9 \times 9 = 81$
$10 \times 9 = 90$
$11 \times 9 = 99$
$12 \times 9 = 108$

Chorus

0 9 18 27 36 45 54
63 72 81 90 99 108
I'm walking on cloud, walking on cloud, walking on cloud nine!

Ten times table time machine

PERFORMANCE **17**   BACKING **18**   **54**

Take a trip on the time machine, counting up the decades as you travel forwards or backwards in time to practise the ten times table.

★ Ask the children what they know about the ten times table. (You add a zero to the number you are multiplying by ten. All the numbers end in zero.) Chant in multiples of ten up to twelve times ten to remind them of the pattern.

★ Display the songsheet (opposite and CD) and listen to performance track 17 to learn the melody:

> *Zero times ten is zero,*
> *One times ten is ten…*

Notice that the rhythm slows from ten times ten to the end.

★ Repeat, singing along with the performance track, then perform with backing track 18 when the children are confident.

WHAT YOU WILL NEED

★ An enlarged version of the songsheet (opposite and CD)

Extension activity:

★ Time machine worksheet (p54 and CD)

EXTENDING THE ACTIVITY

★ Use the Time machine worksheet (p54 and CD) in order to test the children on the ten times table. For the three time machine dials in the left-hand column they will need to work out how many years to travel forwards into the future or backwards in history.

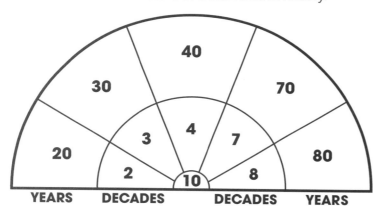

★ Use the blank time machine dials on the worksheet to enter decade numbers of your choice. The children calculate the numbers of years in each decade and write the answers in the outer circle.

Teaching focus
• Learning and exploring the ten times table.

Ten times table time machine

$0 \times 10 = 0$

$1 \times 10 = 10$

$2 \times 10 = 20$

$3 \times 10 = 30$

$4 \times 10 = 40$

$5 \times 10 = 50$

$6 \times 10 = 60$

$7 \times 10 = 70$

$8 \times 10 = 80$

$9 \times 10 = 90$

$10 \times 10 = 100$

$11 \times 10 = 110$

$12 \times 10 = 120$

Legs eleven

Learn this song to memorise the eleven times table and investigate its number pattern.

★ Using a 12 x 12 blank number grid (p55 and CD) ask the children to work out and colour in the number pattern of the eleven times table from 1 x 11 to 9 x 11. What do they notice about the pattern? Can they continue the pattern for 10 x 11, 11 x 11 and 12 x 11?

★ Display the songsheet (opposite and CD) and play performance track 19 to learn the song. Join in with the times table chant and multiples of eleven at the end, using the coloured grid for a visual reminder if needed. When the children are confident, perform the song with backing track 20.

EXTENDING THE ACTIVITY

★ Can the children describe the pattern of increasing numbers from 10 x 11 to 12 x 11 and apply this to work out the next bit of the sequence:

13 x 11 = 143
14 x 11 = 154…

★ Investigate whether a number is a multiple of 11, eg 392601

Add together alternate digits of the multiple:

392601   Add 3 + 2 + 0 = 5
392601   Add 9 + 6 + 1 = 16

If the original number (392601) is a multiple of 11, the difference between these two sums (16 - 5 = 11) will also be a multiple of 11.

Try other numbers to see which ones are multiples of eleven!

WHAT YOU WILL NEED

★ An enlarged copy of the 12 x 12 blank number grid (p55 and CD)

★ An enlarged version of the songsheet (opposite and CD)

Teaching focus
• Learning and exploring the eleven times table.

Legs eleven

Chorus:

With legs eleven the answer's plain,

The ones and tens remain the same,

But after reaching ninety-nine,

Another pattern joins the line.

$$0 \times 11 = 0$$
$$1 \times 11 = 11$$
$$2 \times 11 = 22$$
$$3 \times 11 = 33$$
$$4 \times 11 = 44$$
$$5 \times 11 = 55$$
$$6 \times 11 = 66$$
$$7 \times 11 = 77$$
$$8 \times 11 = 88$$
$$9 \times 11 = 99$$
$$10 \times 11 = 110$$
$$11 \times 11 = 121$$
$$12 \times 11 = 132$$

Chorus

0 11 22 33 44 55 66 77 88 99 110 121 132

Mr Elf

Mr Elf is fascinated by the number twelve, having been born on the twelfth day of the twelfth month! He has a very large family of 144 cousins, and to save him time he counts them in dozens. Learn the twelve times table as you join Mr Elf with his counting!

★ Display the songsheet (opposite and CD) and all chant the vertical number sequence at the end. Can the children identify this number pattern? (It is the multiples of twelve.) Mark the multiples on a 12 x 12 number grid (p55 and CD).

★ Play performance track 21 to learn the song, all joining in with the multiples at the end.

★ Investigate the number pattern of the multiples of twelve and the song's tip for remembering the sequence:

> *Add 2 to the units,*
> *Add 1 to the tens...*

Can the children explain why this rule is different for 60 and 120? (Because 8 plus 2 units equals 10, so you need to carry over the ten.)

★ Learn the whole song, then sing with backing track 22. The children may like to add some simple rhythmic movements to the beat of the music as they sing, eg on the '*Eiy yie yie yie yie*' lines.

WHAT YOU WILL NEED

★ An enlarged copy the 12 x 12 number grid, (p55 and CD)

Extension activity:

★ Mr Elf worksheet (p56 and CD)

★ Colouring pens

EXTENDING THE ACTIVITY

★ Test the children's knowledge of the twelve times table by exploring the things Mr Elf likes to collect. Ask the children to suggest some things he might enjoy collecting and make a list, eg model cars, rings, CDs, hats. He keeps each of his collections in boxes of twelve.

Set some sums for the children to work out using their times tables knowledge, eg
~ How many boxes would be needed for his thirty-six model cars?
~ How many rings has he collected if he has seven full boxes?

★ Can the children colour in Mr Elf (p56 and CD) and design their own illustrations of his collections alongside him, making up sums to test the class?

Teaching focus
• Learning and exploring the twelve times table.

Mr Elf

My name is Mr Elf,
I was born on December the twelfth,
I've one hundred and forty-four
   cousins,
Which I like to count in dozens.

I have a number habit,
One 10 plus 2 ~ I grab it,
I love to search and delve
For those multiples of twelve.

0 x 12 = 0
1 x 12 = 12
2 x 12 = 24
Eiy yie yie yie yie

3 x 12 = 36
4 x 12 = 48
5 x 12 = 60
Eiy yie yie yie yie

6 x 12 = 72
7 x 12 = 84
8 x 12 = 96
Eiy yie yie yie yie

9 x 12 = 108
10 x 12 = 120
11 x 12 = 132
12 x 12 = 144

Add 2 to the units,
And 1 to the tens,
It's easy counting twelves,
When you listen to the elves.
0 12 24 36 48 60 72
84 96 108   120   132   144

Evens

Perform this chant, counting in twos up to one hundred and forty-four, then investigate even and odd numbers.

★ Show the songsheet to the children (opposite and CD). Can they describe the numbers? (They are all even numbers.) Notice the pattern on the songsheet (each vertical column increases in tens).

★ Ensure that the children understand that even numbers are 'evenly' divided by two with none remaining, eg

~ Eight divided by two is four and four with none remaining, therefore eight is even;

~ Seven divided by two is three and three with one remaining, therefore seven is odd.

★ Can they explain why zero is an even number? (Because if you divide it by two you get zero with none remaining.)

★ Play backing track 24 and count in twos from 0 to 144 (all the even numbers, the multiples of the two times table). Notice that after one hundred the counting is slower to fit in all the number words.

★ Now listen to performance track 23. Notice that the male voice highlights the multiples of the four times table over the multiples of two. With the help of the class, colour in the multiples of the four times table on the songsheet. Perform this version using the backing track.

★ Highlight other even number tables using a new copy of the songsheet, eg the multiples of the six times table, and perform with the backing track, then divide into groups to perform with other number tables.

EXTENDING THE ACTIVITY

★ Ask the children to investigate multiplication facts using the multiplication table (p57 and CD). Can they work out rules for multiplying by even and odd numbers? For example, what type of number – odd or even – do you get if you multiply:

even x even (even)
even x odd (even)
odd x even (even)
odd x odd (odd)

WHAT YOU WILL NEED

★ An enlarged version of the songsheet (opposite and CD)

Extension activity:

★ Multiplication table (p57 and CD)

Teaching focus
• Counting in twos.
• Even and odd numbers.

Evens

0	2	4	6	8
10	12	14	16	18
20	22	24	26	28
30	32	34	36	38
40	42	44	46	48
50	52	54	56	58
60	62	64	66	68
70	72	74	76	78
80	82	84	86	88
90	92	94	96	98
100	102	104	106	108
110	112	114	116	118
120	122	124	126	128
130	132	134	136	138
140	142	144		

Multiples of three

Investigate the multiples of three through movement, body percussion and instruments to create musical performances.

★ Make copies of the 12 x 12 grid (p55 and CD) and ask the children to colour in all the multiples of three from 3 to 144: 3 6 9 12… up to 144.

★ Discuss the pattern the multiples have made, eg

~ Straight vertical columns: 3 15 27…
~ Every third number across the grid: 3 6 9 12…
~ Alternate columns of odd and even numbers.

★ Use the coloured grids as a guide, or display the songsheet (opposite and CD), as you join in chanting the numbers with performance track 25.

★ Ask the children to suggest a simple movement, body percussion sound or instrument to play once with each number as they chant. Practise these with the performance track, then perform with backing track 26.

★ Can any children memorise the numbers and perform without following the grid?

EXTENDING THE ACTIVITY

★ Divide the class into two groups. Group 1 chants the three times table multiples with the backing track then group 2 chants the six times table multiples. Group 2 can colour their times table on a separate 12 x 12 grid to use as a guide.

Can anyone predict what the chant will sound like if both groups perform together? (The six times table group will join in on alternate multiples – all the even numbers: 6 12 18…)

★ Allocate sets of instruments to the two groups, eg group 1 plays claves and group 2 plays drums. Perform the two chants together with the instruments.

★ To make the activity more challenging, add a third group – the nine times table. Can the children predict when this group will play? (Every third multiple of the three times table: 9 18 27…) Choose a third set of instruments for this group, eg shakers.

★ Perform all three tables at the same time to create a percussion pattern piece.

WHAT YOU WILL NEED

★ An enlarged version of the songsheet (opposite and CD)

★ Copies of the 12 x 12 grid for each child (p55 and CD)

★ Pens

Extension activity:

★ Claves, drums and shakers

Teaching focus
• Counting in threes.
• Exploring the relationships between the three, six and nine times tables.

SINGING TIMES TABLES BOOK 2 • HELEN MACGREGOR & STEPHEN CHADWICK © 2013 A&C BLACK PUBLISHERS LTD • www.bloomsbury.com/musi

Multiples of three

0

3   6   9   12

15   18   21   24

27   30   33   36

39   42   45   48

51   54   57   60

63   66   69   72

75   78   81   84

87   90   93   96

99   102 105 108

111 114 117 120

123 126 129 132

135 138 141 144

The tables crew

PERFORMANCE **27**   BACKING **28**

Join the tables crew and rap to show that knowing some times tables means we have double the amount of knowledge!

★ Use this rap to explore and remind children of the relationship between tables they already know and tables they are learning, eg the three and the six times tables.

★ Listen to performance track 27 all the way through, then ask the children to explain the maths described in the rap. (If you know the two times table then doubling the answers gives you the four times table and likewise for other tables they know.)

Ask the children if they can think of an easy way to work out, eg 4 x 6, using their knowledge that 4 x 3 = 12.

★ Display the songsheet (opposite and CD) where everyone can see it. Teach the words of the choruses by joining in with the performance track, listening to the examples given between each chorus.

★ Perform the whole rap, including the examples with backing track 28.

WHAT YOU WILL NEED

★ An enlarged version of the songsheet (opposite and CD)

EXTENDING THE ACTIVITY

★ As a class, choose other examples from the tables shown and sing these with the backing track, eg

5 x and 10 x table:	2 x 5 = 10	so 2 x 10 = 20
4 x and 8 x table:	3 x 4 = 12	so 3 x 8 = 24
3 x and 6 x table:	6 x 3 = 18	so 6 x 6 = 36

★ Show the children examples of other ways of using this doubling rule, eg

2 x 4 = 8 so 4 x 4 = 16; 5 x 7 = 35 so 10 x 7 = 70.

★ Divide the class into small groups and select pairs of tables according to their knowledge and ability. Ask each group to make up four new 'doubling' sums for the song to replace the examples given, eg

6 x 4 = 24	6 x 8 = 48	Double it! Double it!
6 x 5 = 30	6 x 10 = 60	Double it! Double it!
6 x 6 = 36	6 x 12 = 72	Double it! Double it!
6 x 10 = 60	6 x 20 = 120	Double it! Double it!

Teaching focus
• Relationships between tables.
• Strategies for multiplication.

The tables crew

We know our tables, we're the tables crew!
Just double the answer, we'll show you!
We know two times, we can work out four,
We know three times, we can work out six.

One times two is two, so one times four is four.
Double it! Double it!
Two times three is six, so two times six is twelve.
Double it! Double it!

We know our tables...
We know five times, we can work out ten,
We know six times, we can work out twelve.

Three times five is fifteen, so three times ten is thirty.
Double it! Double it!
Four times six is twenty-four, so four times twelve is forty-eight.
Double it! Double it!

We know our tables, we're the tables crew!
Just double the answer, we'll show you!
Double it! Double it!

Nine times table finger trick

A rap to help the children use the 'finger trick' method for learning their nine times table before they know it off by heart.

★ Display an enlarged copy of the songsheet (opposite and CD).

★ Demonstrate the finger movements to the children using the finger trick displays (pp58–59 and CD), explaining how they help illustrate the multiples in the nine times table.

★ Play performance track 29 as you all listen to the instructions in the rap and make the matching patterns with the fingers.

★ Learn to say the rap one verse at a time as you perform the finger movements, then join in with the voice on the performance track to perform it all the way through.

★ Perform the whole rap with backing track 30 when the children are confident.

EXTENDING THE ACTIVITIES

★ Show the children the nine times table and ask them to describe any patterns they discover, eg the answer digits always add up to nine:

$$3 \times 9 = 27 \qquad 2 + 7 = 9$$

WHAT YOU WILL NEED

★ An enlarged version of the songsheet (opposite and CD)

★ Finger trick displays (pp58–59 and CD)

Teaching focus
• Method for learning the nine times table.

SINGING TIMES TABLES BOOK 2 • HELEN MACGREGOR & STEPHEN CHADWICK © 2013 A&C BLACK PUBLISHERS LTD • www.bloomsbury.com/mus

Nine times table finger trick

Nine times table ~ rap along,
Remember this trick
   and you can't go wrong!
Hands in front of you, thumbs
   each side,
Let your fingers show the answers
   and be your guide.

Left thumb down, you're doing fine,
That's one times nine is… nine.

Second finger down,
Pointer can't be seen,
That's two times nine is… eighteen.

Third finger down,
Middle's gone to Devon,
That's three times nine is… twenty-seven.

Fourth finger down,
Others straight as sticks,
That's four times nine is… thirty-six.

Fifth finger down,
Baby takes a dive,
That's five times nine is… forty-five.

Right pinkie down,
Bending to the floor,
That's six times nine is… fifty-four.

Seventh finger down,
Got an injury,
That's seven times nine is… sixty-three.

Eighth finger down,
Feeling sad and blue,
That's eight times nine is… seventy-two.

Ninth finger down,
Pointy one has gone,
That's nine times nine is… eighty-one.

Tenth finger down,
Right-hand thumb, yippee!
That's ten times nine is… ninety.

We've run out of fingers,
So make a sign,
Eleven times nine is ninety-nine.
Shake hands with your mate
   and congratulate,
Twelve times nine ~ one hundred
   and eight!

Number lab

Come into the number lab to experiment with number patterns in times tables and discover the relationships between them.

★ Make a large copy of the 12 x 12 number grid (opposite, p55 and CD) and display it where the class can see it.

★ Listen to performance track 31. Three electronic sounds are given at the beginning: a buzz, a beep and a slide down. After the count in, a voice on the track chants the consecutive numbers from 0 to 144, over which the three electronic sounds are heard. Each electronic sound highlights the multiples of its own times table. Notice that after one hundred, the counting is slower to fit in all the number words.

Ask the children to focus on one sound at a time, eg the buzz, to work out which times tables are being used in the lab.
Beep: three times table;
Buzz: four times table;
Slide: eleven times table.

★ Play the performance track again and ask the children to join in counting the multiples of the three times table from 0 to 144. Repeat this for the four times table.

★ Display a large copy of the 12 x 12 grid showing the multiples of three and four (p60 and CD). Divide the class into two groups: group 1 chants the multiples of three and group 2 chants the multiples of four. Investigate the number patterns they can hear using the grid.

★ Ask the children to mark the multiples of eleven on the grid. Now divide into three groups and combine all three tables. Each group chants the multiples of their times table with the performance track 31 to coincide with the matching electronic sound.

★ Choose a body percussion sound for each electronic sound, eg clap, pat knees, swish palms, and perform the combined chants and body percussion in three groups with backing track 32.

WHAT YOU WILL NEED

★ Enlarged copy of the 12 x 12 grid (p55 and CD)

★ 12 x 12 grid showing multiples of three and four (p60 and CD)

★ Individual grids for the class

★ Pens

EXTENDING THE ACTIVITY

★ Perform the three tables with instruments to create a percussion pattern piece:

3 x claves	0	3	6	9	12...
4 x drums	0	4	8	12	16...
11 x shakers	0	11	22	33	44...

Teaching focus
• Practising a times table of your choice.

Number lab

0	1	2	3	4	5	6	7	8	9	10	11	12
	13	14	15	16	17	18	19	20	21	22	23	24
	25	26	27	28	29	30	31	32	33	34	35	36
	37	38	39	40	41	42	43	44	45	46	47	48
	49	50	51	52	53	54	55	56	57	58	59	60
	61	62	63	64	65	66	67	68	69	70	71	72
	73	74	75	76	77	78	79	80	81	82	83	84
	85	86	87	88	89	90	91	92	93	94	95	96
	97	98	99	100	101	102	103	104	105	106	107	108
	109	110	111	112	113	114	115	116	117	118	119	120
	121	122	123	124	125	126	127	128	129	130	131	132
	133	134	135	136	137	138	139	140	141	142	143	144

Rhyme time

PERFORMANCE **33**

BACKING **34**

Use this rhyming song/rap to practise sums from any times tables that the children find tricky to memorise.

★ Display the songsheet (opposite and CD) and play performance track 33 to learn the melody of the sums and the rhythm of the rapped lines.

> Sing: *Eleven times two is twenty-two,*
> Rap: *Lift your arm and touch your shoe.*

★ Play the performance track again and all join in, improvising actions to illustrate the words:

> *Eleven times two is twenty-two,*
> *Lift your arm and touch your shoe…*

★ Divide into two groups to perform the song with backing track 34. Only group 1 is allowed to see the songsheet. Group 1 sings the sums and group 2 responds by rapping the rhymes with actions.

Swap over, so that both groups perform the rhymes from memory.

EXTENDING THE ACTIVITY

★ In two groups as before, reverse the order of the sum and the rhyme. Can group 2 sing the matching sum after hearing the rhyme?

★ Ask the children to identify the sums they have trouble memorising and invent their own rhyming phrases to link with each to help remember them.

Some numbers will not have many rhymes. In this case, make up:
~ Nonsense words which rhyme, eg
  7 x 10 = 70 I know a man called Plevenbee

~ Scat phrases which rhyme, eg
  9 x 10 = 90 n n n, tee hee hee or *shoo shoo shoo whop, doo bee*

★ Turn the rhymes the children have made up into a test by asking them which phrase goes with a particular sum.

Teaching focus
● Memorising tricky tables.

Rhyme time

$11 \times 2 = 22$

Lift your arm and touch your shoe.

$6 \times 6 = 36$

Choose it, choose it, pic 'n' mix.

$8 \times 9 = 72$

Paint your face a vivid blue.

$5 \times 7 = 35$

Lift a leg and do a jive.

$9 \times 11 = 99$

Hang your washing on a line.

$12 \times 12 = 144$

Tap your foot upon the floor.

$9 \times 3 = 27$

Now you're nearly up in heaven.

$4 \times 7 = 28$

Go and lift a tiny weight.

$12 \times 10 = 120$

The money's gone, your wallet's empty.

$8 \times 8 = 64$

Barefoot walk on a sandy shore.

$7 \times 9 = 63$

Climb to the top of a very big tree.

$2 \times 8 = 16$

Make sure your bedroom's very clean.

$9 \times 10 = 90$

Say goodnight: 'Nighty, nighty!'

Rhyme time!

So easy!

Use this song to test children's quick mental recall of any times table they have learnt. The example on performance track 35 uses the five times table.

★ Display the songsheet (opposite and CD). Learn the chorus using performance track 35. Join in with the answers to the multiplication sums in the verses.

★ Choose a times table to test. Substitute questions from that times table for the children to answer in the verses and sing along with backing track 36. Small groups can prepare four sums to make a new verse to test the rest of the class!

EXTENDING THE ACTIVITY

★ Make the test more challenging by mixing up more and more times tables as the children learn them, until eventually you are testing any of the tables they have learnt.

★ Use the test to challenge individual children, eg when lining up to go out to play, give each child a different calculation from a table you know they need to practise.

WHAT YOU WILL NEED

★ An enlarged version of the songsheet (opposite and CD)

Teaching focus
- Mental recall of any times table.
- Understanding uses of times tables.

So easy!
Tune: In dulci jubilo

Chorus:
We know a way to calculate
Inside our heads ~ it's really great!
When we're multiplying
Or when dividing, here's the thing ~
We need to use times tables,
So easy when we sing with rhythm,
We need to use times tables,
So easy when we sing!

Leader:
(Question 1) Four times five is?
(Question 2) And five times five is?
(Question 3) Ten times five is?
(Question 4) Eleven times five is?

Group:
(Answer 1) Twenty.
(Answer 2) Twenty-five.
(Answer 3) Fifty.
(Answer 4) Fifty-five.

Chorus

Leader:
(Question 5) Nine times five is?
(Question 6) And three times five is?
(Question 7) Seven times five is?
(Question 8) Eight times five is?

Group:
(Answer 5) Forty-five.
(Answer 6) Fifteen.
(Answer 7) Thirty-five.
(Answer 8) Forty.

Chorus

Multiply

Learn this rap to help children use and understand the variety of mathematical vocabulary related to multiplication that they need to be familiar with.

★ Learn the rap chorus using performance track 37. Listen to the first verse and the different ways of saying 2 x 5 = 10. Discuss the different vocabulary used. Can the children think of any more ways to describe 2 x 5, eg 'two sets of five'?

★ Listen to the second verse and the other examples.

★ Divide into two groups to perform the verses that give examples of different vocabulary. Display the songsheet (opposite and CD) where everyone can see it.

★ Group 1 sings the first line questions, eg *Two times five. What do you get?* Group 2 answers: *Two times five is ten!*

★ Swap groups for the second verse so that everyone has the opportunity to lead with the questions.

EXTENDING THE ACTIVITY

★ Use backing track 38 to substitute different sums that test the children's multiplication knowledge of the times tables they have learnt.

★ Mix and extend the vocabulary as appropriate, eg 'sets of'. Invite small groups to create a new verse of sums using vocabulary of their own choice.

★ Set problems for individual children to answer using their own choice from the range of vocabulary.

★ Extend the song to explore division vocabulary:

Understanding our times tables,
So many words that you can use,
Shared by, shared between, divided by, into,
We all know what they mean so we can choose!

Ten shared by five. What do you get?
Ten shared by five is two…

WHAT YOU WILL NEED

★ An enlarged version of the songsheet (opposite and CD)

Teaching focus
• Understanding a variety of mathematical vocabulary.
• Recalling times tables.

SINGING TIMES TABLES BOOK 2 • HELEN MACGREGOR & STEPHEN CHADWICK © 2013 A&C BLACK PUBLISHERS LTD • www.bloomsbury.com/mus

Multiply

Chorus:
Understanding our times tables,
So many words that you can use,
Times, lots, groups and multiply,
We all know what they mean
So we can choose!

(Question 1) Two times five.
What do you get?
(Answer 1) Two times five is ten!

(Question 2) Two lots of five.
What do you get?
(Answer 2) Two lots of five make ten!

(Question 3) Two groups of five.
What do you get?
(Answer 3) Two groups of five are ten!

(Question 4) Two multiplied by five.
What do you get?
(Answer 4) Two multiplied by five
  equals ten!

Chorus:
Understanding our times tables,
So many words that you can use,
Times, lots, groups and multiply,
We all know what they mean
So we can choose!

(Question 5) Four times six.
What do you get?
(Answer 5) Four times six is twenty-four!

(Question 6) Five lots of eight.
What do you get?
(Answer 6) Five lots of eight make forty!

(Question 7) Four groups of twelve.
What do you get?
(Answer 7) Four groups of twelve are
  forty-eight!

(Question 8) Three multiplied by nine.
What do you get?
(Answer 8) Three multiplied by nine
  equals twenty-seven!

Chorus

X-men bingo

PERFORMANCE **39**   BACKING **40**   **61**

Use physical movement in the chorus of this rap to reinforce understanding of mathematical symbols and vocabulary then play a bingo game to test times tables knowledge.

★ Choose a times table the children have learnt (the example given on performance track 39 is for the two times table).

★ Learn the actions of the rap together by listening to the performance track. Demonstrate the actions shown opposite and on the bingo actions display (p61 and CD). Hands in the air for 'X-men', use crossed arms in front of the body on 'Multiply', use parallel arms in front of the body for 'Equals', and hands in the air for 'Bingo'.

★ When the children are confident about the actions, add the *X-men bingo* game. Divide the class into teams. Give each child a set of blank bingo cards (p61 and CD) and ask them to complete a card with their own choice of multiples from the two times tables, eg

X-MEN BINGO	
12	20
6	24
4	10

Play the performance track to rehearse the game. At the call section the children mark a cross on their card if they have the matching answer. At the end of the song anyone with all six numbers calls 'X-men bingo!' and that team receives a point.

★ Play the game with backing track 40, starting with a new set of blank bingo cards. In a box or hat, place a set of 13 cards showing each sum for the chosen table (0 x 2, 1 x 2, up to 12 x 2). Choose a bingo caller.

All perform the chorus actions while the caller picks eight cards from the box. At the call section, the caller calls out each sum one at a time. The players mark their cards as before.

Repeat five more times with new numbers and a new caller for each game.

WHAT YOU WILL NEED

★ An enlarged version of the songsheet (opposite and CD)

★ Bingo actions display (p61 and CD)

★ Blank bingo cards (p61 and CD)

★ Pens

EXTENDING THE ACTIVITY

★ Play *X-men bingo* as above to test knowledge of other individual or mixed times tables that the children have learnt.

Teaching focus
- Mathematical symbols.
- Testing any times table.

X-men bingo

Chorus:

We are the X-men, we know the rules,
We're X-perts at our tables,
We're gonna keep it cool!
We need them when we calculate,
We need to know the lingo.
Are you ready? Get your eyes down,
It's X-men tables bingo!

(Question 1)	6 x 2?
(Question 2)	9 x 2?
(Question 3)	3 x 2?
(Question 4)	11 x 2?
(Question 5)	5 x 2?
(Question 6)	7 x 2?
(Question 7)	1 x 2?
(Question 8)	12 x 2?

Chorus:

We are the X-men...

X-men

Multiply

Equals

Bingo

(repeat)

Egg box test

Down on the farmyard the hens are busy laying eggs.
Help to collect and pack the eggs in boxes of dozens.
Use this song to test the children's knowledge of the
twelve times table.

★ Display the songsheet (opposite and CD) and listen to the song and
rap on performance track 41. Can the children listen to the rapped
sums and work out the answer as the hen clucks? After the clucking
'thinking time' the children call out the answer together, eg '*Two
boxes ~ cluck yee ha!*'

★ Ask the children to suggest appropriate movements for the song and
Cluck, yee ha! lines, eg step on alternate feet during the verse then
do hen actions – bend knees with feet out at an angle, flap elbows.

★ Once the children have learnt the song, use backing track 42 to
substitute your own numbers of eggs that need to be packed
into boxes.

EXTENDING THE ACTIVITY

★ Use the twelve times table egg box worksheet (p62 and CD) for
individual children to calculate the answers to other totals, eg 50
eggs (four full boxes and two single eggs). They can colour in the
eggs to show their workings.

★ Give each child a six times table egg box worksheet (p63 and CD).
Using the backing track, test the six times table by packing the eggs
into half dozen boxes and changing the last line of the chorus to:
Six fresh eggs in an egg box… How many boxes do I need?

★ Use the same worksheet (six times table egg box worksheet) to
calculate the answers to other totals, eg 20 eggs (three full boxes
and two single eggs).

WHAT YOU WILL NEED

★ An enlarged version of
the songsheet (opposite
and CD)

Extension activity:

★ Copies of the twelve times
table egg box worksheet
(p62 and CD)

★ Copies of the six times
table egg box worksheet
(p63 and CD)

Teaching focus
• Knowledge of the twelve and six times tables.

Egg box test

We're down on the farm in the early morning
Collecting eggs from the hen house.
In the big red barn we'll pack those eggs,
A dozen eggs fit in an egg box.

(Question 1) Twenty-four eggs to put in boxes,
How many boxes do I need? *(hen thinking time)*
(Answer 1) Two boxes ~ cluck yee ha!

(Question 2) Sixty eggs to put in boxes,
How many boxes do I need? *(hen thinking time)*
(Answer 2) Five boxes ~ cluck yee ha!

(Question 3) Forty eggs to put in boxes,
How many boxes do I need? *(hen thinking time)*
(Answer 3) Three boxes ~ four eggs left!

(Question 4) Seventeen eggs to put in boxes,
How many boxes do I need? *(hen thinking time)*
(Answer 4) One box ~ five eggs left!

Twenty-four eggs divided by twelve is two boxes.
Sixty eggs divided by twelve is five boxes.
Forty eggs divided by twelve is three boxes, four eggs left.
Seventeen eggs divided by twelve is one box, five eggs left.

Rock with three

Air guitar display:

Multiples:	0		3			etc
Consecutive numbers:	0	1	2	3	4	5
	strum	*strum*	rest/air guitar	*strum*	*strum*	rest/air guitar

SINGING TIMES TABLES BOOK 2 • HELEN MACGREGOR & STEPHEN CHADWICK © 2013 A&C BLACK PUBLISHERS LTD • www.bloomsbury.com/musi

Four beat bars

Group 1	Group 2			
0 x 4 = 0	0	0	0	0
1 x 4 = 4	1	2	3	4
2 x 4 = 8	5	6	7	8
3 x 4 = 12	9	10	11	12
4 x 4 = 16	13	14	15	16
5 x 4 = 20	17	18	19	20
6 x 4 = 24	21	22	23	24
7 x 4 = 28	25	26	27	28
8 x 4 = 32	29	30	31	32
9 x 4 = 36	33	34	35	36
10 x 4 = 40	37	38	39	40
11 x 4 = 44	41	42	43	44
12 x 4 = 48	45	46	47	48

0   4   8   12   16   20   24   28   32   36   40   44   48

Four beat bars

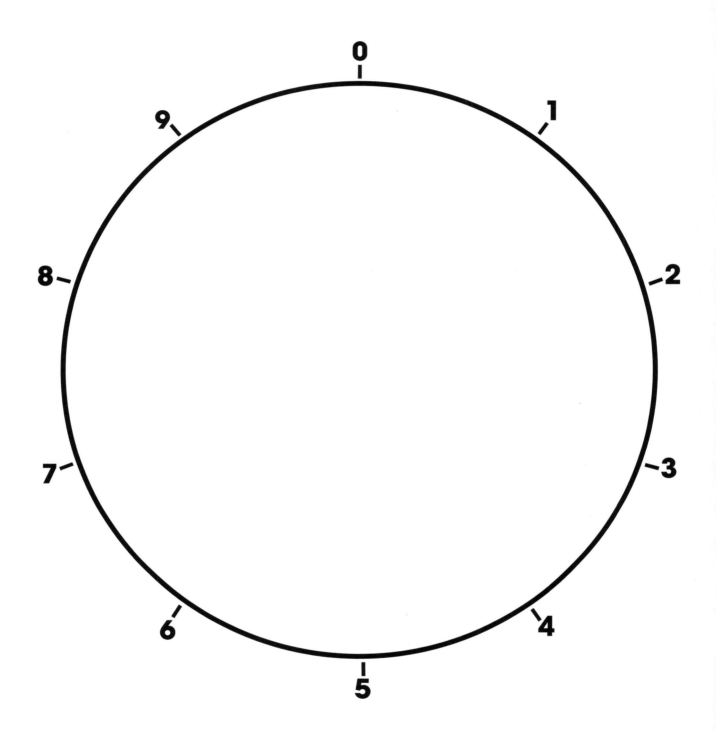

SINGING TIMES TABLES BOOK 2 • HELEN MACGREGOR & STEPHEN CHADWICK © 2013 A&C BLACK PUBLISHERS LTD • www.bloomsbury.com/musi

Seven days a week

Week	Monday	Tuesday	Wednesday	Thursday	Friday	Saturday	Sunday
1							
2							
3							
4							
5							
6							
7							
8							
9							
10							
11							
12							

Seven days a week

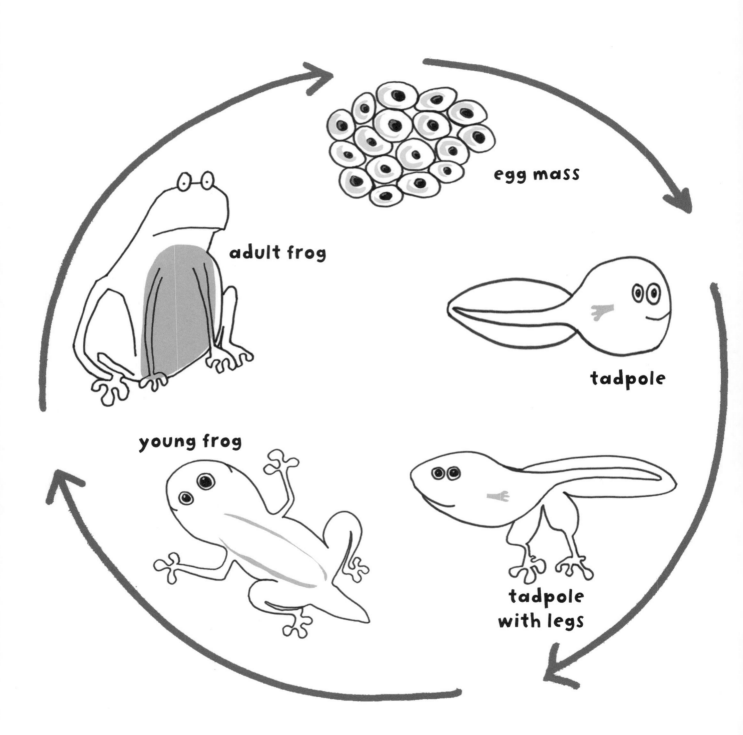

egg mass

adult frog

tadpole

young frog

tadpole
with legs

SINGING TIMES TABLES BOOK 2 • HELEN MACGREGOR & STEPHEN CHADWICK © 2013 A&C BLACK PUBLISHERS LTD • www.bloomsbury.com/mus

Octopi

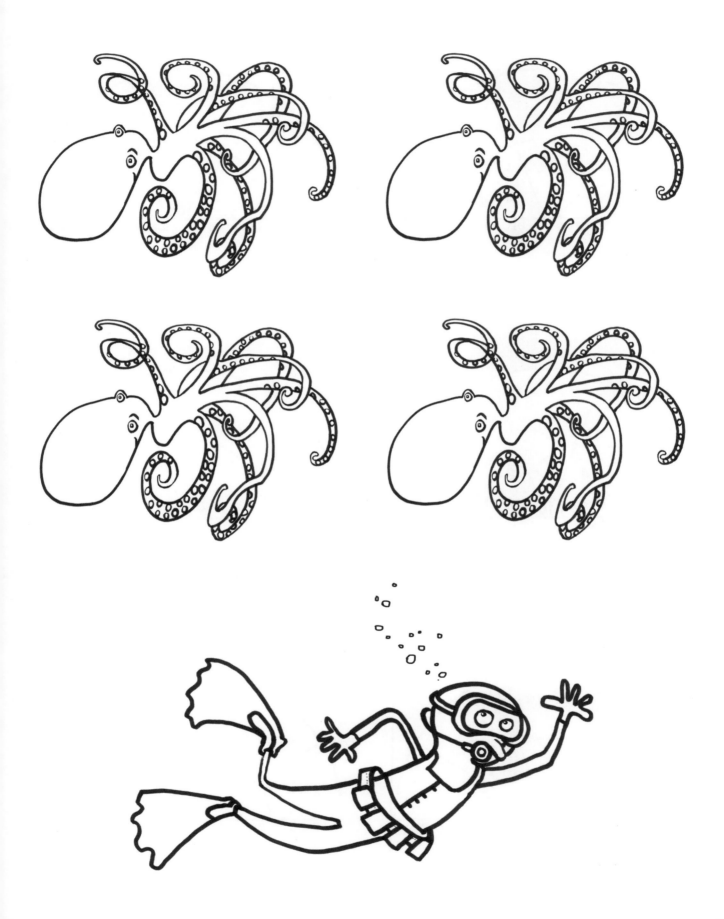

Ten times table time machine

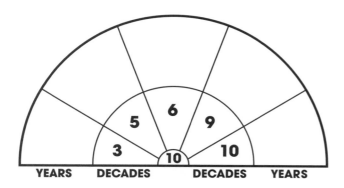

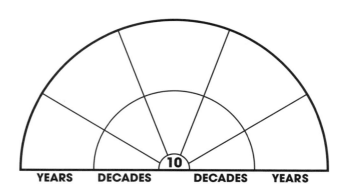

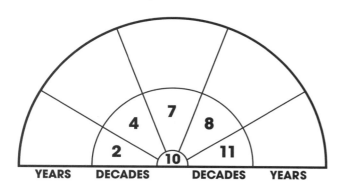

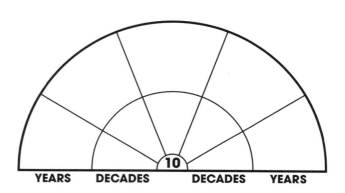

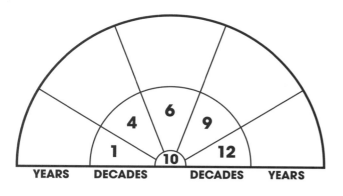

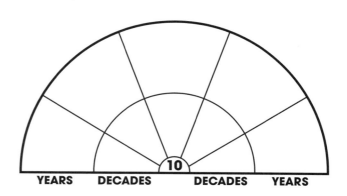

12 x 12 grid for Legs eleven, Mr Elf, Multiples of three, Number lab

1	2	3	4	5	6	7	8	9	10	11	12
13	14	15	16	17	18	19	20	21	22	23	24
25	26	27	28	29	30	31	32	33	34	35	36
37	38	39	40	41	42	43	44	45	46	47	48
49	50	51	52	53	54	55	56	57	58	59	60
61	62	63	64	65	66	67	68	69	70	71	72
73	74	75	76	77	78	79	80	81	82	83	84
85	86	87	88	89	90	91	92	93	94	95	96
97	98	99	100	101	102	103	104	105	106	107	108
109	110	111	112	113	114	115	116	117	118	119	120
121	122	123	124	125	126	127	128	129	130	131	132
133	134	135	136	137	138	139	140	141	142	143	144

DISPLAYS, TEMPLATES AND WORKSHEETS

Mr Elf

Evens

×	1	2	3	4	5	6	7	8	9	10	11	12
1	1	2	3	4	5	6	7	8	9	10	11	12
2	2	4	6	8	10	12	14	16	18	20	22	24
3	3	6	9	12	15	18	21	24	27	30	33	36
4	4	8	12	16	20	24	28	32	36	40	44	48
5	5	10	15	20	25	30	35	40	45	50	55	60
6	6	12	18	24	30	36	42	48	54	60	66	72
7	7	14	21	28	35	42	49	56	63	70	77	84
8	8	16	24	32	40	48	56	64	72	80	88	96
9	9	18	27	36	45	54	63	72	81	90	99	108
10	10	20	30	40	50	60	70	80	90	100	110	120
11	11	22	33	44	55	66	77	88	99	110	121	132
12	12	24	36	48	60	72	84	96	108	120	132	144

SINGING TIMES TABLES BOOK 2 • HELEN MACGREGOR & STEPHEN CHADWICK © 2013 A&C BLACK PUBLISHERS LTD • www.bloomsbury.com/music

Nine times table finger trick

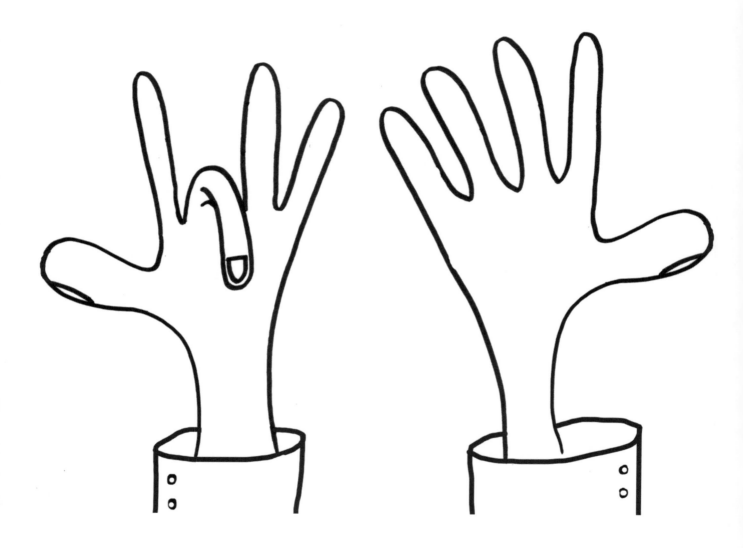

Third finger down,

Middle's gone to Devon,

That's three times nine is... twenty-seven.

SINGING TIMES TABLES BOOK 2 • HELEN MACGREGOR & STEPHEN CHADWICK © 2013 A&C BLACK PUBLISHERS LTD • www.bloomsbury.com/music

Nine times table finger trick

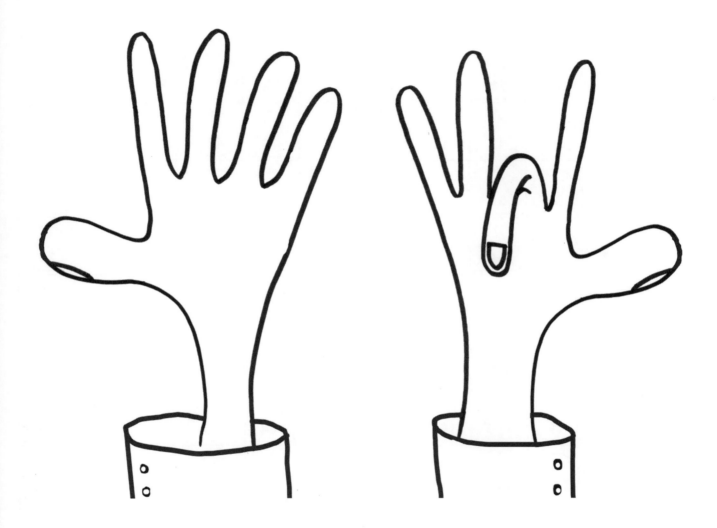

Eighth finger down,

Feeling sad and blue,

That's eight times nine is... seventy-two.

Number lab

1	2	3	4	5	6	7	8	9	10	11	12
13	14	15	16	17	18	19	20	21	22	23	24
25	26	27	28	29	30	31	32	33	34	35	36
37	38	39	40	41	42	43	44	45	46	47	48
49	50	51	52	53	54	55	56	57	58	59	60
61	62	63	64	65	66	67	68	69	70	71	72
73	74	75	76	77	78	79	80	81	82	83	84
85	86	87	88	89	90	91	92	93	94	95	96
97	98	99	100	101	102	103	104	105	106	107	108
109	110	111	112	113	114	115	116	117	118	119	120
121	122	123	124	125	126	127	128	129	130	131	132
133	134	135	136	137	138	139	140	141	142	143	144

◯ Multiples of three   △ Multiples of four

SINGING TIMES TABLES BOOK 2 • HELEN MACGREGOR & STEPHEN CHADWICK © 2013 A&C BLACK PUBLISHERS LTD • www.bloomsbury.com/musi

X-men bingo

X-MEN	BINGO

X-men:

Multiply:

Equals:

Bingo:

Egg box test (twelve times table)

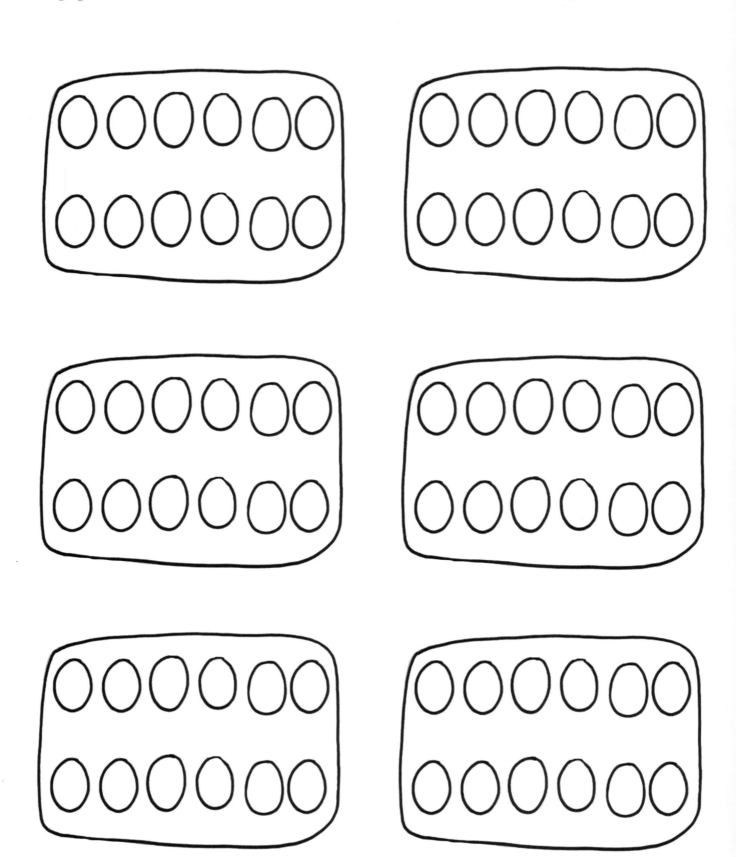

SINGING TIMES TABLES BOOK 2 • HELEN MACGREGOR & STEPHEN CHADWICK © 2013 A&C BLACK PUBLISHERS LTD • www.bloomsbury.com/musi

Egg box test (six times table)

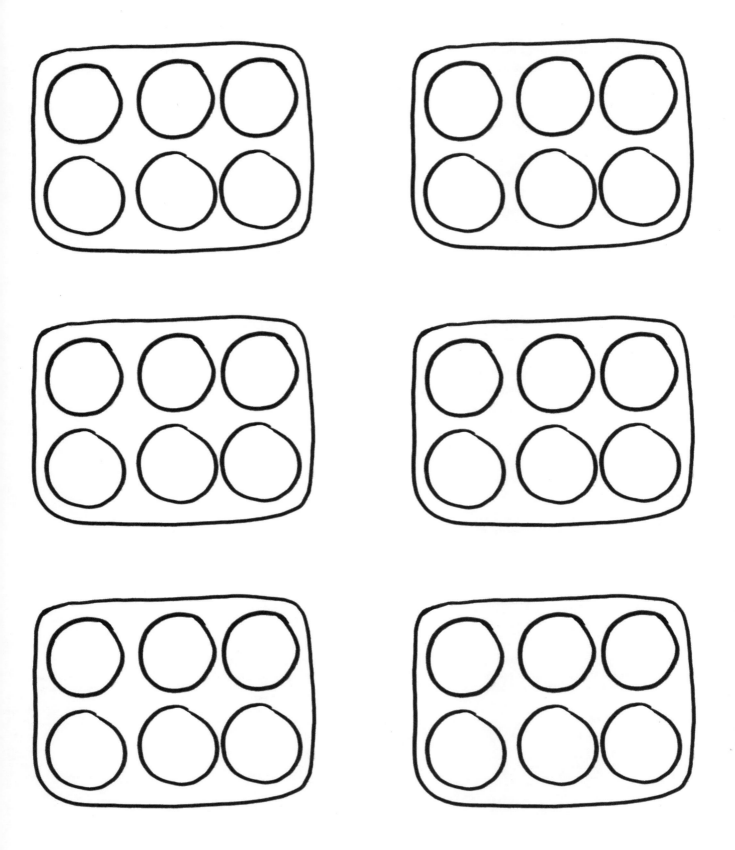

Song index and track list

First published 2013 by A&C Black Publishers Ltd
Bloomsbury Publishing Plc, 49–51 Bedford Square, London, WC1B 3DP
© 2013 A&C Black Publishers Ltd
ISBN 10: 1-408194362
ISBN 13: 978-1-4081-9436-2

Text copyright © 2013 Helen MacGregor, Stephen Chadwick
Songs copyright © 2013 Helen MacGregor, Stephen Chadwick
Edited by Sheena Roberts and Stephanie Matthews
Cover illustration © 2013 Julia Patton
Inside illustrations © 2013 Julia Patton
Vocals performed by Sian Jones and Nigel Pilkington
Backing tracks by Stephen Chadwick
Sound engineering by Stephen Chadwick
CD post-production by Ian Shepherd, Mastering Media
Designed by Jocelyn Lucas
Printed by and bound by CPI Group (UK) Ltd, Croydon, CR0 4YY

Acknowledgements
Thanks to Anna, Sheena Roberts, Chris Hussey and Michelle Daley.